GROUND CONTROL TO MAJOR TIM

THE SPACE ADVENTURES OF MAJOR TIM PEAKE

CLIVE GIFFORD

WAYLAND

www.waylandbooks.co.uk

First published in Great Britain in 2017 by Wayland
Copyright © Wayland, 2017

Editor: Nicola Edwards
Design: Smart Design Studio
Cover design: Lisa Peacock

ISBN: 978 1 5263 0095 9
10 9 8 7 6 5 4 3 2

MIX
Paper from
responsible sources
FSC® C104740

Wayland, an imprint of
Hachette Children's Group
Part of Hodder and Stoughton
Carmelite House
50 Victoria Embankment
London EC4Y 0DZ

An Hachette UK Company
www.hachette.co.uk
www.hachettechildrens.co.uk

Printed and bound in China

Picture acknowledgements: The publisher would like to thank the
following for permission to reproduce their pictures: ESA Cover
(background), 5, (top right), 12, 28, 14-15; /Stephane Coraja, 2015:
Cover (main), 14, 28-9; /M. Koell: 9; /A. Le Floch: 11 (right); /H. Rueb,
2010: 11 (left), 13 (right); /Philippe Sebirot, 2015: 6L; ESA — handout/
Getty Images18-19, 21 (top right), 24-5, 27; ESA/NASA: 17B, 20,
21B, 22, 23, 25T, 26; Jack Taylor/Getty Images: 8 (left); NASA: 1, 2, 5
(bottom), 16, 17 (top); 18, 19, 25 (bottom); /Bill Ingalls: 29; /Joel Kowsky:
3, 4; /Robert Markowitz: 6 (right); /Bill Stafford: 10; /Viktor Zelentsov: 13
(left), 15 (top right); Shutterstock 7, 8 (top).

CONTENTS

Welcome to Space, Major Tim 4

Dreams of Flight 6

In Service 8

Years of Training 10

Preparing for Principia........................... 12

Blast Off!.. 14

Life Onboard 16

Tim at Work 18

The Experimental Astronaut......................20

Spacewalk 22

Downtime in Space 24

Marathon Man 26

Welcome Home, Major Tim 28

Glossary..30

Further information 31

Index...32

WELCOME TO SPACE, MAJOR TIM

On 15 December 2015, Major Tim Peake found himself over 400,000 m above the Earth's surface. While Britain's Helen Sharman had visited the Mir space station in 1991, Tim was the first official British astronaut in more than two decades and the very first to visit the biggest, most advanced machine in space – the International Space Station (ISS).

Tim was taking part in ISS Expedition 46, during which he would spend over six months in space. First there was the tricky matter of reaching and docking with the ISS. This was no easy task when the ISS was whizzing through space on its orbit around Earth at a ferocious speed of 27,580 km/h – travelling over 7.6 km every second.

Tim Peake (bottom), Tim Kopra and Yuri Malenchenko give a final wave before climbing into their Soyuz spacecraft bound for the ISS.

MISSION MEMO

ISS FACT FILE
FIRST LAUNCHED: 1998
LENGTH: 109 m
MASS: 419,725 kg
TYPICAL CREW: 6
ISS ASTRONAUTS (2000-MID-2016): 222
POWER: 8 solar panels generating 84 kilowatts

Cool under pressure

Beside Tim in the cramped surroundings of the Soyuz capsule (below) were two crewmates, mission commander Yuri Malenchenko and Tim Kopra. Malenchenko had already spent 461 days in space on five separate missions. He had to call on all this experience when the KURS radar system, used in docking the spacecraft with the ISS, failed. Back on Earth, Tim's family and friends could only watch the nail-biting scene as Malenchenko skilfully took control of the Soyuz craft and carefully docked the spacecraft by hand.

After over two hours of checks performed by Tim and his crewmates, and some 8 hours and 22 minutes after leaving Earth, airlock hatches opened and the three space travellers entered the ISS. Tim was welcomed by Scott Kelly (right), the mission commander of the previous ISS mission, Expedition 45. Later he enjoyed his first meal in space – a bacon sandwich washed down with a cup of tea.

> "It was a beautiful launch. The first sunrise was absolutely spectacular, and we also got the benefit of a moonrise which was beautiful to see."
>
> Tim Peake

DREAMS OF FLIGHT

How did Tim become Britain's first European Space Agency (ESA) astronaut and find himself orbiting 400 km above Earth?

Timothy Nigel Peake was born in Chichester on 7 April 1972, just three years before the ESA was founded. His school reports describe him as calm and level-headed, and his parents marvelled at his determination to keep practising things he was interested in until he mastered them. Whether it was running, exploring the countryside or performing science experiments, Tim enjoyed a challenge.

Tim's official portrait after he joined the European Space Agency (ESA).

Tim's father, Nigel (right) and mother, Angela (left) greet Tim at Cologne, Germany on his return from his mission into space.

Soldiers march at Sandhurst Academy in Surrey. Training is mentally and physically demanding for recruits intent on becoming officers in the British Army.

Sparking a passion

Tim's father, Nigel was a journalist with a strong interest in aviation. He took Tim to a number of airshows where historic and current aircraft gave displays. Tim soon became hooked on aircraft, especially helicopters. In his teens he joined the Combined Cadet Force (CCF), where he learned all about aircraft. His interest in space was ignited when he read about the 1969–72 Apollo missions to the Moon.

In control

Tim took his A Levels knowing he wanted to be a pilot, ideally of helicopters. By the age of 18 he had already notched up 40 flying hours with the CCF. These included 10 hours solo when he had complete control of the aircraft.

Adventures in Alaska

At the age of 17 Tim gained a place at the Royal Military Academy Sandhurst to train to become a member of the British Army. Before he started there, his thirst for adventure took him on a three month trip to Alaska. He was part of an Operation Raleigh expedition, mapping parts of Alaska's remote coastline by canoe and studying salmon populations. Conditions were tough and very cold, but as Tim wrote on the Operation Raleigh website, "Living in harsh, demanding conditions makes for a great expedition – otherwise it's just a holiday."

"Tim was a bright, charming, hardworking student. He was an excellent team player even in those days, and was of course good at his physics." Mike Gouldstone, Tim's high school physics teacher

IN SERVICE

After graduating from Sandhurst, Tim served as a platoon commander in the Royal Green Jackets before becoming an officer in the British Army Air Corps. He qualified as a pilot in 1994 and over the next decade served in warzones including Afghanistan and Bosnia as well as in Kazakhstan, Canada, Kenya, Northern Ireland and Germany.

While serving at the British Army base in Gütersloh, Germany, Tim met Rebecca King (below, with Tim), also an army officer. The pair married in 2000 in St Andrews, Scotland, and shortly afterwards, moved to the United States. There, Tim learned to fly Boeing AH-64 Apache helicopters with the US Army. He became a highly skilled and experienced Apache pilot and then, in 2005 moved into work as a test pilot. A year later, he completed a science degree in Flight Dynamics and Evaluation from the University of Portsmouth.

An Apache helicopter is packed with technology and weapons. When British forces chose to equip themselves with 67 of these advanced attack helicopters, Tim helped develop the overall training plan as well as instructing new pilots.

Major Tim

By 2009, Tim, now a major in the Army, had logged over 3,000 hours piloting a wide range of aircraft and helicopters. He decided to retire from the Army as he saw his likely career path in the military taking him out of the cockpit and into management. He preferred to continue flying, and a new job in 2009 as a senior test pilot with AgustaWestland allowed him to do just that ... until Tim received an incredible message from the European Space Agency ...

Fateful phone call

Back in 2008, Tim had applied along with 8,412 others for one of the six places on offer by the ESA to train to become an astronaut. In a process lasting almost a year, Tim had to answer round upon round of online questionnaires, face-to-face interviews, tests and medical and psychological evaluations. Gradually, the numbers of applicants were whittled down, first to 918, then 192 and finally, 22. Tim made it to the 22 but then heard nothing for weeks until he received a life-changing phone call from the ESA on 18 May 2009. He had been selected as one of the six! He told the BBC that this "was the pinnacle" of his career.

The ESA's six new astronaut candidates in 2009: back row left to right Tim Peake, Andreas Mogensen, Alexander Gerst, Luca Parmitano and front row Samantha Cristoforetti and Thomas Pesquet.

MISSION MEMO

Today's astronauts are drawn from many different occupations, but in the early days of spaceflight most of the candidates were military pilots. It was thought that pilots of fast jets would have the experience of high G forces and the reactions and skills to do well in space. All 20 of the first trainee astronauts of the Soviet Union (known as cosmonauts) were pilots. In 1961, Yuri Gagarin was selected from this group to become the first person to travel into space.

YEARS OF TRAINING

Becoming an astronaut is no easy task. The years of training demand dedication and sacrifice, not just by the astronauts themselves but by their families, too. Tim and Rebecca had just had their first son, Thomas, but there was no time to relax and enjoy family life. They moved to Cologne, Germany, home of the European Astronaut Centre. There Tim would begin some 14 months of intensive general training.

Tim had vast amounts of technical information about spacecraft and their equipment to take in. He also had to learn about space engineering and emergency medicine and perform hundreds of practice drills.

Patient and determined, Tim took most of his training in his stride, although he did struggle with one element – learning the Russian language. This was necessary because much of the hardware used to launch astronauts into space, as well as many of his potential fellow astronauts, come from Russia.

Tim (right) and Tim Kopra undergo emergency training in a smoke-filled mock-up of part of the International Space Station. Astronauts have to be prepared for every eventuality.

A world of work

Tim's training took place all over the world, from the European Astronaut Centre to Star City in Kazakhstan and from the Tsukuba Space Centre in Japan to the Johnson Space Center in Houston, Texas. At the headquarters of the Canadian Space Agency in Quebec, Tim practised controlling a mock-up of the large robotic arm fitted to the space station used to retrieve satellites and other objects in space.

Tim's training took him to some unusual places. He and other trainee astronauts were sent to Sardinia to live underground in caves for a week. In Kazakhstan, Tim learned how to survive should his returning space capsule land in water or a snowy forest.

In 2012, Tim even spent 12 days underwater as part of NASA's Extreme Environment Mission Operations (NEEMO) mission. This involved living in Aquarius, a base 20 m below sea level off the coast of Florida.

SPACE SCIENCE

The 'Vomit Comet' is the nickname given to a large aircraft that performs a series of sharp dips and climbs to simulate short periods of reduced gravity. The sensation created is close to the feeling of weightlessness that astronauts experience in space. The nickname comes from the sickness some have to deal with as they float inside the aircraft.

Tim experiences weightlessness on board an Airbus A300 Zero-G in 2010 next to EAC Instructor Gail Iles.

Tim anchors himself underwater during the NEEMO mission so that he could collect samples without drifting away.

"You're up there by yourself. There's no doctor, there's no computer engineer – so you have to learn all of these skills."
Tim Peake speaking to the BBC

PREPARING FOR PRINCIPIA

Being an 'unassigned' astronaut with no specific mission to train for can be hard. So Tim was understandably overjoyed to learn in May 2013 that the uncertainty was over. He had been assigned a mission – a six-month stay on board the International Space Station beginning in 2015. The mission would become known as Principia.

Tim now had to get to grips with all the elements that his long mission in space would involve. He practised training drills for emergency situations and learned how to support crewmates on an Extra Vehicular Activity (EVA) or spacewalk.

Tim had to get to know every aspect of the International Space Station and its workings, as well as the Soyuz spacecraft that would ferry him and two crewmates from Earth to the ISS. During his mission Tim would perform more than 30 advanced science experiments, and he had to familiarise himself with all these before he left.

Tim tests out an Airway Monitoring machine. This measures and analyses gases that astronauts breathe out to help check on their health.

Tim is fitted for his spacesuit before his mission.

SPACE SCIENCE MISSION MEMO

NASA's Neutral Buoyancy Laboratory in Houston, Texas, contains the world's largest swimming pool. This 62 m-long, 31 m-wide, 12.34 m-deep tank holds an incredible 23.5 million litres of water – enough to fill more than 100,000 bath tubs – and contains a full-size replica of the International Space Station. Astronauts wear neutral buoyancy suits, similar to spacesuits but with weights so that they don't rise or sink but float underwater where they can simulate spacewalking tasks.

Plenty of practice

There was every chance Tim's mission would include an EVA of his own. EVA training takes place underwater to mimic the microgravity of space. Tim trained in special pools in the United States, Germany and Russia. This involved gruelling underwater sessions in a full spacesuit, often for six hours at a time, practising all the tasks involved in a long spacewalk.

Excitement builds

Nothing is left to chance on a major space mission. Tim's health and fitness were monitored frequently and he was measured for his purpose-built suit and seat on the Soyuz spacecraft. He had to make many decisions, including choosing his meals on board the ISS months in advance. It was an exciting time for Tim, and he couldn't wait for 15 December 2015 – launch day – to come.

Tim (right) gets to grips with working underwater in a neutral buoyancy tank in preparation for his EVA in space.

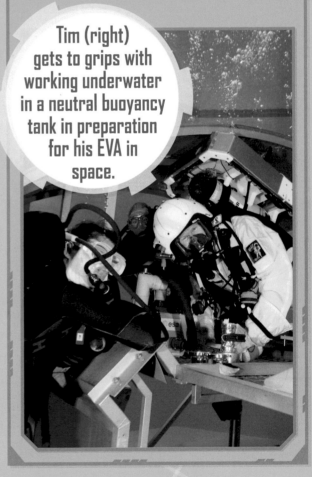

"Every spacewalk is carefully planned and rehearsed ... we practise the whole sequence in a pool several times."
Tim Peake, interviewed in *Engineering and Technology* magazine

BLAST OFF!

With a final clanging sound, the hatch to the Soyuz TMA-M was shut and sealed. There was no turning back now.

Tim, Yuri Malenchenko and Tim Kopra were strapped into their custom-made seats on top of a 49.5 m tall Soyuz FG rocket. This 305,000 kg beast takes around one and a half hours to fill with fuel which it burns fiercely to generate the vast amounts of power required to overcome Earth's gravity and head into space.

Goodbye and good luck!

Two hours earlier, Tim had waved goodbye to his wife Rebecca and his two sons, Thomas and Oliver, from behind a glass screen (below). The three astronauts had been put in quarantine so that they do not carry bugs into space or pick up a last-minute cold or virus. Their day had begun some eight hours before launch, with final medical checks, travel to the launch site (left) and getting into their pressurised spacesuits before the big blast off into space.

Left to right: Tim Peake, Yuri Malenchenko and Tim Kopra

MISSION MEMO

Each of the three astronauts picked three songs which were played inside the Soyuz spacecraft in the 40 minutes before launch time. Tim chose *Don't Stop Me Now* by Queen, *Beautiful Day* by U2 and Coldplay's *A Sky Full Of Stars*.

Once inside their spacecraft, large numbers of safety checks helped pass the time and ease the nerves, but still, as a first-timer, Tim had to call on all his military training to stay calm and focused. At last, the launch sequence entered its final seconds and the engines fired with an enormous roar – sending a low rumble through the Soyuz cabin.

A roaring success

"The whole ride into space on the Soyuz rocket was so powerful," noted Tim. And no wonder, with the four 19.5 m tall booster rockets helping to generate 422.5 tonnes of thrust at launch – around 18 million cars' worth of power. The four boosters only burn for 118 seconds before they fall away, and the launch vehicle's core engines take over.

Now Tim and the others were over 35 km above the Earth's surface, hurtling at speeds of 5,390 km/h. After 8 minutes, 48 seconds, Tim experienced a shuddering jolt as the Soyuz spacecraft, now 210 km above Earth, separated from the remainder of the rocket. It would now cruise through space to reach its destination.

Expedition 46's astronauts stand in front of the Soyuz capsule in which they will travel to the ISS.

Expedition 46 blasts off from Baikonur. The Soyuz FG rocket burned 270 tonnes of fuel in just 8 ½ minutes during launch.

"I mean that must have been the most perfect lift-off – the weather, the view, the sky and then the condensation cloud. It was just magical."
Nigel Peake, Tim's father, speaking to the BBC shortly after the launch

SPACE SCIENCE

As there is no air or oxygen in space, rocket engines must carry their own supply of oxygen or oxidiser (oxygen-making chemicals). This is pumped into a combustion chamber where it is mixed with kerosene fuel, ignited and burned, creating huge amounts of rapidly inflating gases. These escape from the rocket engine via its exhaust nozzles, thrusting the launch vehicle in the opposite direction with much power – Tim's Soyuz FG went from a standstill to around 1,700 km/h in just 60 seconds.

LIFE ONBOARD

After such a long and eventful day to get to the ISS, Tim expected to sleep well. But even though he had trained in simulators that mimicked microgravity, he still had to get used to securing himself inside a sleeping bag and fixing it to the wall or ceiling of the Harmony module.

Without Earth's gravity to act as a guide, it can be hard for new arrivals on board the ISS to keep their balance. But by Tim's second full day aboard his body had adjusted. He also had to get used to seeing the 16 sunrises and 16 sunsets the ISS crew experience every 24 hours, as the space station completes an orbit of Earth every 90 minutes.

Space Science

The ISS was built piece-by-piece in space. Its construction took more than 110 spaceflights and dozens of spacewalks. It consists of a long spine called a truss, fitted to which are science, docking, storage and living modules and four giant pairs of solar arrays. The space station has provided a continuous home to astronauts since 2000.

Zvezda

Zarya

Tranquility

Destiny Lab

Kibo

Harmony

Columbus European Lab

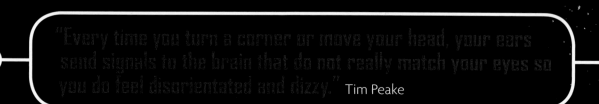

"Every time you turn a corner or move your head, your ears send signals to the brain that do not really match your eyes so you do feel disorientated and dizzy." Tim Peake

Everyday life and extraordinary scenes

The ISS has the same amount of living and working space as a five- or six-bedroomed house. It's also warm (18–27°C) and quite noisy with all the machinery and cooling fans whirring round. Tim's training meant he was soon able to find his way round its modules and corridors. He knew that absolutely everything, from a tool to a toothbrush, had to be fixed in place to stop it floating away.

The space station's modules are pressurised with air to breathe, so Tim could work in shirt sleeves and no spacesuit. With no laundry in space, clothes are worn on average for 10 days at a time. Drinking water is recycled from the space station's two toilets. Tim knew all these facts in advance, but one thing his training hadn't prepared him for was how stunning the views of Earth would be, or for "when you look in the opposite direction and you see how dark space is. It is just the blackest black".

Tim (here in the Cupola of the ISS) was in charge of 2 kg of rocket plant seeds which were used in an experiment to learn about how microgravity affects plant growth.

MISSION MEMO

Two of the astronauts that greeted Tim and the other arrivals in December 2015 hold the record for the longest single stay on the ISS. Mikhail Korniyenko and Scott Kelly spent 340.4 days aboard the ISS between March 2015 and 2016.

Tim finished work around 7 p.m. most evenings, but his working day began about 12 hours earlier. Alarms sound and lights are turned on at 6 a.m. After freshening up and breakfast, the crew contact mission control for an early morning conference to discuss the tasks they are to perform. In Tim's experience, no two working days on the ISS were quite the same.

Much of Tim's time was spent working on a huge number of different experiments (see pp20–21), but other tasks included regularly cleaning the interior of the space station and shifting and cataloguing supplies. There were maintenance tasks too, from replacing air filters to repairing machinery. With no gravity, dust floats throughout the ISS and can clog filters and equipment. Cloths and a special vacuum cleaner are used to collect as much dust as possible.

Tim carries out an experiment in the Harmony module of the ISS.

Careful manoeuvres

Tim was tasked with launching DIWATA-1 – the Philippines' first ever satellite – which will be used to monitor the environment and forecast the weather. He worked with flight controllers in Japan to launch the satellite from the Kibo module.

Tim also helped to deploy the Bigelow Expandable Activity Module (BEAM) on the ISS (below). This flat-packed giant inflatable had to be taken out of a supply spacecraft and attached to part of the space station. It would later be inflated with air to provide extra work or storage space.

A tricky task

Unmanned spacecraft bring supplies to the ISS and take away waste. In April 2016, Tim took on one of the hardest tasks: free flyer track and capture of the supply spacecraft.

Using two hand controllers to move a large robot arm, he had to catch the SpaceX Dragon spacecraft as it travelled 10 m below the ISS and then attach it to a node on the Harmony module. "In case this all sounds too easy," Tim said in an interview, "there is also a 90-second time limit – and failure is not an option!"

Tim controls Canadarm2 to capture the Dragon spacecraft carrying three tonnes of food, supplies and new experiments.

MISSION MEMO

Tim used social media to answer questions about his work on board the ISS. His Twitter account had 825,000 followers by the end of his mission.

THE EXPERIMENTAL
ASTRONAUT

The main purpose of Tim's mission was to carry out more than 200 science experiments that could only be performed in space.

The experiments were very varied. Tim used a mini furnace called the Electromagnetic Levitator (EML) to study metals at high temperatures (over 2,000°C) in a floating environment. The SPHEROIDs experiment studied how the cells that line human blood vessels react to living in space. Tim trialled the Vessel ID system, designed to track as many as 22,000 ships as they sailed Earth's seas and oceans. He tested out breathing in the ISS's airlocks and recovered bacteria and fungi after they'd spent a year in space in the Expose-R2 experiment fitted to the outside of the space station.

According to Tim, "the coolest experiment was actually looking at flame combustion". This used the Combustion Integrated Rack (CIR) found in the Destiny laboratory on the ISS to burn materials in space and study their effects.

Tim at work beside the Combustion Integrated Rack in the equipment-packed Destiny laboratory.

Roving robot

As part of the ESA's Meteron project, Tim had the chance to control a robot on Earth while he was on the ISS. He used joysticks to navigate a 1.65 m-long, six-wheeled robot rover called Bridget (right) around a yard full of rocks and sand. The yard simulated the surface of Mars but was actually located in Stevenage in Hertfordshire! The aim of the test was to trial new technologies that may enable future astronauts orbiting the Moon or Mars to use robots to explore the surface below.

"The science being studied on board the Station is incredibly exciting and has the potential to deliver major breakthroughs in several areas, such as medical treatments, new materials and our fundamental knowledge of the universe." Tim in the Principia science brochure

The human body in space

Tim himself was the subject of experiments designed to learn more about human health and the effects of space on the human body. The Skin-B experiment, for example, measured and monitored Tim's skin to detect aging and any health issues. The MAREs machine gathered regular information about the strength of his muscles to provide data about muscle wastage in space. Tim's eyes, brain and immune system were also monitored and measured while he was on board the ISS.

Among the many experiments performed on Tim himself was the use of this fundoscope to measure eyeball and vision changes in space.

SPACEWALK

> ## "Popping outside for a walk tomorrow."
> **Tim's** tweet on 14 January 2016

In December 2015, Tim had supported two of his crewmates, Scott Kelly and Tim Kopra, while they performed a spacewalk. On 15 January 2016, Tim finally got the chance himself to step outside the ISS and head out into space to perform an EVA (Extravehicular Activity) alongside his crewmate, Tim Kopra.

Careful checks

Preparations had begun several weeks earlier. Every movement and task outside had to be memorised, and detailed checks made to space suits and all the equipment and tools the astronauts would use. The very first spacewalk, performed by Alexei Leonov in 1965, lasted just 10 minutes, but the two Tims' EVA was scheduled to take more than six hours, so there was a lot to learn – the document of instructions was 40 pages long!

Coverings on helmet visor protect Tim's eyes from the Sun's harmful UV rays.

Like all astronauts, Tim doesn't eat on a spacewalk but can sip water through a straw inside his helmet.

Suit made from 14 layers to protect against tiny particles whizzing through space. Called micrometeoroids, these could rip through flesh.

Oxygen and radio contained inside Primary Life Support System (PLSS) worn as a backpack.

Gloves feature tiny heaters to keep Tim's fingers warm.

Cooling system inside suit includes liquid-cooled underwear.

SPACE SCIENCE

Tim's spacesuit protected him from many threats in space, such as temperatures varying from 120°C in direct sunlight down to -160°C in darkness.

Into the airlock

Once in their spacesuits, the two astronauts entered the Quest airlock on the station. Here they spent two hours breathing pure oxygen to remove all the nitrogen from their bodies. This was to stop them getting 'the bends' – similar to when a deep sea diver surfaces too quickly – in their pressurised spacesuits. Finally, Tim headed out into space.

An important task

The main task was to replace a failed Sequential Shunt Unit (SSU) – an electrical box which helps control power generated by the ISS's eight giant solar panels. Tim had to carry the replacement on a challenging journey, using his arms to clamber 50 m along one of the trusses that form the ISS's frame to the very edge of the space station.

Tim's spacewalk was cut short a little but lasted 4 hours, 43 minutes , during which time the ISS orbited the Earth three times. The ISS was back on full power as a result of the successful mission for the first time since November 2015.

Tim could light up his immediate working area with lights in his helmet.

MISSION MEMO

There have been 193 spacewalks so far to build or look after the International Space Station. These total 1,204 hours, 48 minutes in space. The longest spacewalk of all was performed by Susan Helms and James Voss in 2001 and lasted 8 hours, 56 minutes.

"Today's exhilarating spacewalk will be etched in my memory forever – quite an incredible feeling!" Tim Peake

DOWNTIME IN SPACE

In his spare time, Tim enjoyed reading and listening to music. He could watch movies on laptops, and got to see *Star Wars: The Force Awakens* projected onto a screen hung up on one of the space station's walls.

One of Tim's favourite things to do was simply to take in the view from space, especially from the panoramic Cupola with its seven windows perched on top of the Tranquility module. Armed with a digital camera, Tim snapped hundreds of photos of space and the Earth's surface, many of which he shared online. Tim also used the Internet link from the station to stay in contact with his family and keep up with the news.

Tim is a big fan of sports and keeping fit. One of his treats when living on the ISS was to have a rugby union game from the Six Nations competition in February 2016 beamed to the space station so that he could watch it live.

Mealtimes

Food for astronauts started out as unappetising cold pastes in tubes or dried into cubes. Meals on the ISS are hot and more varied than in the past. They are carefully designed to be healthy and nutritious and not to allow crumbs or liquids to float around the spacecraft. Many foods are freeze-dried to save weight with hot water added in the space station's galley. Tim was excited to receive some meals prepared by celebrity chef, Heston Blumenthal, including beef truffle stew, key lime pie and a turkey dinner shaped like an astronaut's helmet for Christmas Day, followed by Christmas pudding.

Tim demonstrates what happens to food in microgravity on board the ISS.

Dinner time ISS style! Tim has a meal with Tim Kopra (left) and Jeff Williams (centre) in the Unity module.

MISSION MEMO

The crew had a guitar with them on board the ISS (although Tim admitted he only knew how to play a few songs). He and Scott Kelly even got to play a virtual space invaders game. This was after they'd experimented with a serious task, Project Sidekick, to create a virtual reality world that would allow mission control staff on Earth to work alongside astronauts on the ISS.

MARATHON MAN

In 1999, Tim had run his first London Marathon, completing the 42.2 km-race in three hours, 18 minutes and 50 seconds. His second London Marathon attempt was going to be out of this world ... literally.

Astronauts suffer from the effects of microgravity when they spend long periods in space. Their muscles are not put under the same loads and strains as they are on Earth with its strong gravity. Without intensive exercise, their muscles can start to shrink in size with a loss of strength and function. As the heart is a large muscle, cardiovascular fitness is also an issue.

Space Science

Long periods spent in space and especially microgravity affect the human body in a number of ways. Most of these effects can be reversed after time back on Earth.

FACE: With next-to-no gravity, body fluids aren't pushed down and float inside the body leading to a puffy neck and face.

EYES: Some astronauts report vision problems on longer missions. Scientists think it may be due to pressure on the brain and optic nerve that carries signals from the eye.

MUSCLES: Some muscles can shrink between 20 per cent and 50 per cent on long missions if astronauts don't exercise regularly.

SPINE: With gravity not pressing the vertebrae of the spine downwards, astronauts can grow 5-8cm while in space.

BONES: Astronauts lose calcium and between 1-2 per cent of their bone mass for every month they stay in space.

Exercising on the ISS

Regular, prolonged exercise in space helps to reduce the effects of microgravity. ISS astronauts workout for up to two and a half hours every day. They use specialised gym equipment including a strap-in cycle machine and a special weights machine called ARED (Advanced Resistive Exercise Device). ARED uses air pressure rather than heavy metal weights to force the astronaut's muscles to work hard.

A marathon effort

Tim's marathon attempt took place in the Tranquility module on the T2 treadmill. A series of elastic straps acted as a harness to keep Tim on the treadmill. Before his space marathon, Tim was linked to the start line in London and provided a countdown for the more than 39,000 runners on the ground. He used an iPad app which gave him a digital view of his progress while he watched live TV footage of the race. Despite the harness beginning to rub and chafe some 40 minutes into the run, Tim completed the marathon in three hours, 35 minutes and 21 seconds. This was an impressive effort considering he was 17 years older than at his first attempt. Even more impressive was the overall distance he had covered, as during his run the ISS had travelled an incredible 86,000 km through space.

Tim during his marathon on the ISS. He attached a water pouch to the ceiling using Velcro strips and could watch the race on the ground via a TV link as he ran.

MISSION MEMO

Tim's marathon was the second performed in space. The first was by female astronaut, Sunita Williams on the ISS in 2007. Sunita completed her marathon on a different treadmill to Tim's in a time of four hours, 24 minutes.

WELCOME HOME, MAJOR TIM

On 18 June 2016, Tim headed home. His historic mission had lasted 186 days. During this time the ISS had made 2,976 orbits of Earth and travelled a distance of some 125 million km. That's more than 162 round trips from Earth to the Moon and back!

The journey home was in the same Soyuz TMA-M craft that had brought the two Tims and Yuri to the ISS over six months earlier. The descent took a little over three hours. At first the spacecraft edged away gently from the ISS at a speed of 10 cm per second. Once clear of the space station, the Soyuz gave a burst of its thrusters to travel further away, then fired its engines fully for more than four minutes to power its descent. It reached a speed of around 28,000 km/h – 25 times the speed of sound.

> "Best ride I've been on, ever."
> Tim Peake, describing his journey back to Earth

Farewell, gentlemen

Tim had felt like an ISS veteran when he said his goodbyes in early March to the three members of the ISS crew who had greeted him when he arrived the December before. Now it was his turn to leave, waved off by the three remaining members of Expedition 47 and with new ISS commander, Jeff Williams ringing a bell and saying, "Soyuz-TMA departed. Farewell, gentlemen, see you on the ground."

Re-entry

The craft used the friction it encountered when re-entering the Earth's atmosphere as a brake to slow itself down. This friction generates large amounts of heat. The craft's exterior glows white hot as temperatures reach over 1,700°C. Inside the 2.2 m-wide craft, the rapid slowing down pressed the astronauts back into their seats with forces around five times that of Earth's gravity.

Back with a bump

About 15 minutes before landing, a small parachute (called a drogue) opened, followed by a larger one to slow the craft down further, with six small thrusters firing just before impact. A strong wind led to a bumpy landing, and the module came to rest on its side in a field in Kazakhstan. The three astronauts were carried out of the module by a recovery team.

Before being whisked away for medical checks and a reunion with his family, Tim gave his first thoughts on his incredible mission: "It's just been fantastic, from start to finish ... I'm just truly elated, just the smells of Earth are so strong, it's wonderful to be back."

"I would go back in a heartbeat."
Tim Peake

SPACE SCIENCE

Like all returning ISS astronauts, Tim had to contend with a readjustment period on Earth. Most feel weak, heavy-limbed and unsteady, and have periods of dizziness, vertigo and feeling faint, partly caused by low blood pressure. Tim had to train hard to regain strength in the months following his return. It's not just physical; Tim's moods and emotions were monitored as he became used to life back on Earth and his newfound celebrity.

GLOSSARY

airlock
A compartment or chamber on space stations and spacecraft sealed by two doors in which changes in air pressure can be managed.

aviation
A term used to describe the design, building and use of aircraft such as military jets and airliners.

cardiovascular
To do with the heart and blood vessels in the body. Cardiovascular fitness is the ability to exercise for long periods of time during which your heart and blood vessels supply your muscles with oxygen-rich blood.

deploy
To place in position and make ready for operation.

EVA
Short for Extra-Vehicular Activity and commonly known as a spacewalk, this is when an astronaut heads outside of their spacecraft to perform tasks in space.

friction
A force between two surfaces that are sliding, or trying to slide, across each other. Friction usually generates heat and slows the movement down.

graduating
To successfully complete and pass a training course or academic course.

microgravity
The very weak pull of gravity experienced by astronauts in space.

modules
Sections of the space station which are launched separately and then fitted together in space.

neutral buoyancy
A situation where someone or something is as dense as the water surrounding it, so that it neither sinks nor floats to the surface.

orbit
To travel around another object in space in, usually, an elliptical shaped path.

panoramic
A sweeping wide view.

psychological
All about the state of mind and emotions of a person.

quarantine
To place a person or other living thing in isolation, away from others, to prevent them either catching or spreading disease.

radar
A system of detecting objects in the air or space using radio signals which are sent out and bounce back off objects.

replica
An exact model or copy of something, such as a space capsule for astronauts to train in.

satellites
Moons or human-made machines which move in an orbit around a planet.

simulate
To imitate something such as to use models to imitate certain tasks that have to be performed by astronauts in space.

solar arrays
Large panels of photovoltaic cells which convert light from the Sun into electricity.

Soyuz
The name of a family of Russian (and in the past Soviet Union) spacecraft, which carry up to three astronauts and supplies into space.

test pilot
A skilled and experienced pilot who flies new, experimental aircraft, testing them out.

vertigo
The feeling of your surroundings spinning around you, sometimes leading to dizziness and potential loss of balance.

> "To make a career in space you should be passionate about what you do, study hard and persevere to make your dreams come true."
>
> Tim Peake

WEBSITES

www.esa.int/esaKIDSen
The kids' webpages of the European Space Agency (ESA) are packed with fun and fascinating facts about life in space.

principia.org.uk
The official website for Tim's Principia mission contains lots of information, interviews and links to other sites.

www.bbc.co.uk/guides/zq3hycw
A guide to how Soyuz crews re-enter the Earth's atmosphere and land back on the planet.

www.bbc.co.uk/guides/zxk7tyc
A guide to how rockets propel craft into space, presented by Tim.

astro-pi.org
Learn more about the Astro-Pi experiments designed by schoolchildren which Tim performed in space.

http://tinyurl.com/qcn8j58
Check out a series of 360° panoramic photos taken by Tim of his training on the ground in different parts of the world.

http://tinyurl.com/huvgoeh
NASA's webpages on the International Space Station for students are full of helpful resources.

ONLINE VIDEO

http://tinyurl.com/zb3lurd
The ESA's video channel is packed with videos showing Tim at work and play on the ISS.

www.bbc.co.uk/newsround/36560356
See Tim's top ten moments in space in short video clips, brought to you by CBBC Newsround.

https://youtu.be/WkYz43qALMU
A 10 minute video tour of the International Space Station conducted by former station commander, Mike Fincke.

BOOKS

Watch This Space: Astronomy, Astronauts and Space Exploration – Clive Gifford (Wayland, 2015)

How To Design The World's best Space Station - Paul Mason (Wayland, 2016)

Go Figure: A Maths Journey Through Space - Anne Rooney (Wayland, 2014)

The Story of Space Stations - Steve Parker (Franklin Watts, 2015)

What's Next? The Future Of...: Space Exploration - Diane Bailey (Franklin Watts, 2013)

INDEX

airlocks 5, 20, 23
Alaska 7
aviation 7
Bigelow Expandable Activity Module (BEAM) 19
Blumenthal, Heston 25
Canadian Space Agency 11
Earth 4, 5, 6, 12, 14, 15, 16, 17, 20, 21, 23, 24, 25, 26, 28, 29
Earth's atmosphere 28
Earth's gravity 14, 16, 26, 29
European Astronaut Centre 10, 11
European Space Agency (ESA) 6, 9, 21
Expedition 46 4, 15
experiments 6, 12, 20, 21
Extra Vehicular Activity 12, 13, 22, 23
Gagarin, Yuri 9
Germany 8, 10, 13
G forces 9
helicopters 7, 8, 9
Helms, Susan 23
International Space Station (ISS) 4, 5, 12, 13, 16, 17, 18, 19, 20, 21, 22, 23, 24, 25, 27, 28, 29
Japan 11, 19
Johnson Space Center 11
Kazakhstan 8, 11, 29
Kelly, Scott 5, 17, 22, 25
Kopra, Tim 5, 14, 22
Korniyenko, Mikhail 17
landing 29
launch 5, 13, 14, 15
Leonov, Alexei 22
London Marathon 26, 27
Malenchenko, Yuri 5, 14

Mars 21
microgravity 13, 16, 26, 27
Mir space station 4
Moon 5, 7, 21, 28
NEEMO mission 11
Neutral Buoyancy Laboratory 13
orbit 4, 16, 21, 23, 28
parachute 29
Peake, Nigel (father) 6, 7, 15
Peake, Tim
   as subject of experiments 21
   astronaut 4, 5, 6, 9, 10, 13, 14, 22, 28, 29
   at Royal Military Academy Sandhurst 7, 8
   born 6
   celebrity 29
   completes science degree 8
   crewmates 5, 12, 14, 22, 25, 28, 29
   in Royal Green Jackets 8
   joins Combined Cadet Force 7
   major in British Army 9
   marries Rebecca King 8
   onboard the ISS 16, 17, 18, 19, 20, 21, 24, 25
   on social media 19
   Operation Raleigh 7
   parents 6
   pilot 7, 8, 9
   returns to Earth 28, 29
   runs marathons 26, 27
   school 6, 7
   serves in warzones 8
   sons 10, 14
   spacewalk 12, 13, 16, 22, 23
   training 10, 11, 12, 13, 15, 17
Philippines 19

Principia mission 12, 13, 21
Project Sidekick 25
quarantine 14
radar 5
readjustment 29
recovery team 29
robot rover (Bridget) 21
Russia 10, 12
Russian language 10
Sardinia 11
satellites 11, 19
Sharman, Helen 4
songs 14
Soviet Union 9
Soyuz capsule 5, 12, 13, 14, 15, 28
Soyuz FG rocket 14, 15
spacesuits 13, 14, 22, 23
Tsukuba Space Centre 11
United States 8, 13
Voss, James 23
Williams, Sunita 27